OFFERINGS TO A TUMBLED TEMPLE

by
Leticia Urieta

**Purple
Ink Press**

San Diego,
California

Purple Ink Press
6977 Navajo Road, Unit 414
San Diego, California, 92119
www.purpleinkpress.com

Offerings to a Tumbled Temple / Leticia Urieta. -- 1st ed.
ISBN 979-8-9892793-5-7

Cover image by Yael Aldana
Cover design and interior design by Yael Aldana

To Ramiro, my love and partner through all the joys, the heartaches, the surgeries, the tears and laughter. You've been there for it all and I love you for walking this path with me.

To all of the women in my family who encouraged my words and my connection with my body, especially my grandmothers Paula and Ines, my cousins Beth and Trisha, my aunt Sherri and my mother Christi.

"The kingdom of the ill is mighty and legion, and it is the borderland all bodies must pass through. And we have set up tents, encampments, and homes. We wave at you from beyond the gates.

When you have arrived, you have arrived. Welcome and blessings."

-*Pain Woman Takes Your Keys, and Other Essays From a Nervous System*

by Sonya Huber

«Table of Contents»

Altar

You, with your back bent,
became the mountain pass.
We used your spine,
bent as it was towards your work,
and made your ridges into footholds,
climbing towards the other side.

You could not follow to the other side
just as now we bend towards your image
adorning you with flowers
in our dreams
la corona de la muerte
I see you asleep with the stars.

Asleep with the stars,
your body stone,
built on ancestral columns,
cracks rivering up your legs
in raised blue that marks you as
mother.

Mother, giver,
broken before time.
The in between must be a relief,
a crescent moon cradles your tired back
and you are out of reach.
We cannot claw you back down.

We cannot claw you back
into our life's blood,
pooling thick and brown

in the crags and fissures,
the pillar and bowl
of our family altar.

Our family alters futures
and relives pasts.
I wish for you a hummingbird,
a portal to return,
and yet no return
from guiding the sun home.

Keep Safe

How best may I honor You?

What you ask me—
lay bare on the altar my most precious memory
us reunited
cut from my mind with the ceremonial blade
obsidian and jade
bifurcate and search out the organ of truth

You are who I lay myself bare for
let scorpions hang off my face for
let my body become a garden for
surrender to your will

Your blade bisects
rends muscle flayed open
fibrous tissue rebuilding protein
Your absence a cauterized wound
of misunderstandings

In the bowl I burn your image for cleansing-
Three sweaters, you were always cold
the black gold ring you never found
newspaper clippings of houses never lived in
dog figurines you said I would
like these ashes I smear on my cheeks
my chin
over my eyes
in remembrance of a life lived and
returned to dust.

I trapped your words in a jar to keep them

from the sucking maw
of a world that could never hear you   that devours the words of
wordless women
words rattle in the jar like so much unused currency

The final rite-
lift the jar's lid and
suck your words in
let them sift and settle in my mouth,
keep you in my lungs for a while and
see which ones I can use to
breathe back into the world

Questionnaire from your in-laws after ten years away

It's good to see you,
did you lose weight?
Did you gain weight?
Why do you eat so little?
Are you sick?
You should eat more,
it's not healthy not to eat.
Here, I am serving you a plate.
Why don't you make his plate?
You must like to study all the time,
you're always reading.
What are you studying for?
Do you even work?
Why do you wear your hair like a boy?
You don't like makeup?
I've never seen you wear makeup.
I like your tattoo.
You know what the bible says about...
You'd be prettier if you...mi linda preciosa.
So you don't want kids,
or you can't have kids?
Why haven't you had kids?
We love you.
Don't come back without a baby on your hip.
Two would be better.
What took you so long to come back?
Why haven't you come sooner?
If you came sooner, Abuela
would be serving you this plate.
Abuela would be making fresh cheese
and tortillas in the clay oven.
Abuela would be here to embrace

you and fill your ear with her laugh.
She wanted to say goodbye one last time before she passed.
Have you gone to see her grave? Come, up the hill
to the panteón to pay your respects.

Swipe your hand across the marble stone, light a new candle for her, sit
in the heat and watch the sun go down around us. See our footsteps.
Press your hand to the earth and remember that we have been waiting
to see what you will do. Now, take care of one another, off in that
lonely country. Fold our words into your clothes. Your maleta is
heavier now with all the things we wanted to give you.

Nerve

is to have grit to stand near the fire

without fear of burning / but all I do

is burn and pulse / after the trauma

after the moment my protective sheath

was damaged / when something unknown

pressed against me in the dark and / hurt me

now / all the messages sent along

my body are abnormal / static in a telephone line

my body is functional / no doubt there

but to say that I am sensory is vital too

the parts of me that branch

into different directions are purely sensory

and / why is this considered weak?

That I feel / flare in distress

when under attack is natural

as the neurons flowing through me

saying / something doesn't feel right

I'm sorry there are no discernible triggers

that my warnings can be ignored / until

I am shouting underneath your skin and you

and still expect to feel or chew or blink

and I hope you remember when you

clench your jaw against the pain that you know
I do that too.

Pain scale

Rate your pain on a scale of–

1. A parachute fallen in the shaded woods
2. Cutting heirloom tomatoes for a salad. The fleshy pale red   center reminds you of the inside of your uterus which was scraped clean of the remnants of a pregnancy. They taste acidic, blood in your mouth
3. Complete relief of sweat cooling in the middle of your back
4. A bunch of silky rosemary cut with care from the bush growing wild
5. Deepest burning breath before the undertow pulls you back
6. Losing the dexterity of your tongue over a word you no longer recognize, choking on your own spit
7. A plastic prescription bottle that rattles with the last pill inside
8. Pasture green amazonite warming against the throat
9. The delicious rot as you stand over the compost and pour more slimy potato skins and banana peels in to witness the hopeful decomposition that will feed all the creatures you cannot see
10. The crumple of translucent examination table paper under your bare ass. You are afraid to hear it move and wrinkle under you, even knowing how it will be torn away and discarded

Walking in the woods with pain

I have not made a hospitable home full of tinctures and rinses and
screams echoing off the empty walls that rise and fall around her   I
have tried to make it as unwelcome as possible
but she remains squatting, insistent laying her coal fire hands on my
nerves in hopes of making a cold hallow warm   She has forgotten the
way out of my body has forgotten a time when she didn't make a home
in me   each time she takes my hand and leads me forward   knocks me
down   She has taught me to forget a time before being on my knees
face to the earth, twigs and leaves plastered to my cheeks by sticky
predictable spit and tears   I was led there under the pretense of relief
while she filled my coat with rocks and whispered 'soon you will be
strong enough to fly'   We meet in the woods, which in the day can
be hopeful whose light can be a glory and at night, she leads me away
from the edge where people offer rescue, medicine and cures   She has
taught me to distrust the promises of strangers   We walk together
forgetting cracking sticks under our boots   I know her names, they are
tattooed on my tongue—sting, burn, pulse, cry, ebb, flow, blood, dry,
tears, gasp, vomit, gulp, bile, moan—these and more I am still learning
to say to love the body where pain walks   lost in the woods of me

A Complete Narrative of My Body to Give My Doctor (s) At Our First Meeting

After Torrin A. Greathouse

What seems to be the issue?

Dr. _____ (redacted), my body is an
abacus clicking one wooden bead at a time to cause a reaction
bent on further destruction, until all the beads slide to one side,
clacking into place like a capsizing ship
drowning under the weight of too much imbalance, too many new medications
eclipsing the brain. The nerves swell, shout, fracture open the air,
fog the brain. I can see across dimensions if I stare long enough through the
gaps that open and close the world like lungs gasping.
Haze, struggle to understand the sensory input of a world waking to its
inheritance of dirt. Sorry, I was only
joking, the world will never see. They don't know how to plant the dead
kingdom, or learn from the earthworm passing through the soil,
loosing two paths inside of them
moving in opposite directions for the good of regeneration.
Needle pierces the estuaries of my blood to search for questions
owed my blood, the vials discarded in another
place, a river flowing with what once flowed in me turned to clotted secrets
quantified only by data on my phone, hours slept, how many days in pain

release the numbers in hopes of a new story and I am still scared of what they will do with it. I wish for my body to make its transformation, a shapeshifter that will finally give up and takes its final form. Become something viable instead of ever vigilant wondering what ailment can be divined from xylomancy, messages from the wood rot of my own yearning, and at the end I am asked to deliver myself to the zealots of "*anything can be cured with time.*"

Safety Summary—an erasure

(Purpose)
      Medicine is used for
      Medicine is taken
      this dose, your last dose

(Warnings)
      Do you tell your doctor if
      you are safe?
the ingredients may cause
      emergency
      get help, right away
      for your face, mouth, tongue or throat

(Learn More)
      about this medicine
      every time
      Your Doctor is the best person—
      Your cost is subject to the usual charges

This offer is,
in whole or in part,
void
without notice

An Exercise in Astral Projection

Keep my body close
hang your leg over my belly,
tethered to the bed,
my consciousness narrows to breathing
through this moment
the pain makes me levitate,
it lays me bare, rips me open until
pain is just a word, a promise under the skin,
both happening and not
all I want is to leave
my body with you, trusted beloved,
while I float out of me,
press pause on the agony, and drift
watching your glorious arms around me
my own face clenched, sweating
 I leave pain in my body and fly
away over my city, over parks, rivers,
cars stuck in traffic
people dancing, kissing
over a mountain.
I fly myself any place where pain can't make me
forget my own name
brush my ghost fingers through creek water,
the swaying hair of a stranger
the feathers of a hawk in flight
 I will come back only when the coast is clear
when the tears on my face have dried to salt
against your lips, when relief is in sight
but not yet arrived, I will lay back into myself,
closing the escape hatch behind me, only remember—
relief is the name of every loving lie we tell

What greater love than refilling a pill organizer?

Tip each long pill down the hill   of my hand to be deposited
in each miniscule box   some to be picked up between two fingers
with tenderness lest they fall   on the bedsheets or on the floor
(they will and I will pick them up, say "five second rule," dust my breath across their
surface and we will never speak of how you are anointed by my breath)

What relief, to know what you need to swallow   for each day,
even for each hour, the pills no longer   sequestered in their bottles
affixed to names, side effects   when you get to a certain age
you grow accustomed to letting others worry for you about "why so
many, and what for?"

I have done this refilling for many elders   the act inconsequentia
but vital though I will leave and someone else will have to take down the plastic
casements and do this prayer   all over again   the pills a rosary we say every day,
running our thumbs across their glistening surfaces, reminding me of beads I kept
in plastic boxes   as a child all shining, some metal and even precious glass to twine
on thin strings   as gifts for my friends

Now, I have my own box of weekly relief, choosing a Sunday,
how appropriate, to fill   each day with remedies   my tried and true   My box is
not yet elaborate   but it is purple,
a light royal color for a kindness from my past self   beginning again
with each   empty   box

Spell for Healing

Oil from an unwashed face
Skin from worrying your bottom lip
Nails that carry the world underneath
them
Sweat collected from between your
thighs
Your arms your breasts your neck
Your first silver hair curled around your
Finger and the clumps from the drain
Swipe a drop or two of blood
Wherever you find it pooling
Blow your nose into an empty cup
Stir the viscera with your finger
they all go into the same pot
but be careful not to leave it
lying around for someone to use
against you
Boil it all down to an elixir of gold
and remember that all the parts
you so easily throw away
still carry their prayers for you

A Year of Offerings to the Body

On the first day
I laid down a golden gift at her altar
believing that glitter would appease her

On the second day
I brought her vials of fragrant oils
she could bathe in
they only lasted for a while

On the third day
I gave her a bowl of fire
that mimicked the waving flames of her eyes

On the fourth day
I left a jug of spring water at her feet
the kind that washes away sins

On the fifth day
I showed her a mirror
to call her back to herself

On the sixth day
I broke a painted pot at her feet
and rubbed the dust on my face to hide from her

On the seventh day
I carried a basket of snakes to her doorstep
She wanted to be closer to power

On the eighth day
I carved the ancient blade across my skin
let blood dribble across her toes
believing there was an exchange

On the ninth day
I clutched the hem of her skirt and sang
like the morning birds at her window

On the tenth day
I stayed away
there is hope in holding my breath

On the twentieth day
I lay my head on her knees and cried
wondering if tears would satiate her thirst

On the fiftieth day
I beat my chest and screamed at her
not once did she smile

On the hundredth day
I tried it all over again

On the two hundredth day
I sat next to her chair and took her hand in mine

On the day I stopped counting
I told her I was ready to listen

The Graveyard of Good Health

Here is the dirt where I am born
And here is the hole where I step
Into the moonlight beyond the graveyard
of good health where I let my comforts
die and grow into pale roses that bloom
in the star's glow-that cry for color
and a kiss from the sun's honey spit
There is moon energy in my face
in my eyes and in my teeth and in my
blood and if I planted my still bloody baby
teeth in the graveyard of good health
they would sprout dewy tears from my
mother when I throw out the parts that are
no longer useful but that she loved

A grave for my teeth
A grave for a still, calm heart
A grave for nerves free from pain
A grave for blood that knew when to flow
and when to clot

That did not rot in the hollowed passages
and infect the body with a sense of longing
for a day when pain is a wave receding-
it crashes against the seawall inside
spills over and around the sides
The moon controls my tides

A grave for my need
A grave for letting it get
the better of me.

I lie on hallowed ground
spread out in a starfish pose

ready to sink through the grass
and acidic graveyard soil to get to all the parts of me
buried,
eager to see
what can grow

Advice in preparation to hold life

She said she couldn't bear to wear shoes, that she had to be bare foot, like no other time before or since, her feet nestled to cold tile or hot earth to feel things growing against her skin, to feel the creature growing inside and know it was hers. She said she gave up the ashes on her fingers, the smooth, stinky smoke flowing from her lips, just like that. There was struggle to reach for a slim candle, to see the paper burn up before her eyes, to feel autonomous from the body inside the body. "I did it for you," she says.

What they can't say—how the body can grow and change without you, your body is now a place of becoming, the whorls and ridges of baby's fingerprints, their identity in this world created from them pushing against your body. That is the most uncertain time, when you know how little you cared for yourself until you had to be a home for someone else, when you too are becoming a home for beautiful things.

Beating Heart

after Kim Sousa

This body is an insurmountable debt
the balance too big to ever pay back

is that why I've never seen a heart beat?
The third time my body has swollen,

begun to prepare a way, my heart is a live wire,
unprotected from its own corrosive sweet hope.

At the 7 week ultrasound, I wait for this tool
of divination to reveal the fetal movement

where cells amass in incomplete possibilities,
and when the doctor says there is no growth

the almost baby frozen in time,
was that body's the bill come due?

After two other losses, I knew to expect the worst
of a life never—

If life begins at conception, is this baby the
living dead, a miracle soon to be flushed from

my body? If life begins at the first biblical breath,
I put the pregnancy test next to the other two

before to keepsake my body's best efforts to make
fertile a fragile, clinging, wanting womb.

Fuck Doctor Strange, a person pregnant
is a better interdimensional traveler in

just one body, able to imagine infinite possibilities
they may never touch, no certain futures

a tidal of blood, the body cut open
a cry, a breath, are all equally possible impossibilities.

Weeks later and I burn with missing
someone I never got to meet,

though relief lives there too, that I didn't
let my love for this almost baby grow

past its own 7 weeks (what a beautiful lie)
that my body can be mine alone again,

but little one, I was ready to give it up,
to be fed on and flayed open to your love

to let my body grow past its own limits.
There were no guarantees we would both make it out

alive. I wonder, walking back to my car from
the clinic sweating through the forty-fifth day

of 105 degrees without rain in a tight mask,
leaving the receptionist who wore her mask

below her nose in a mockery of "care,"
how was I ever to keep you alive on this side?

Being pregnant is to inhabit the most radical hope
that somehow this will be different, that you

could protect your baby with only your fearsome
bloody love, like throwing stones in the raging fire

of your own heart.

In gratitude for color contrast

The red smile
of the cardinal's flitting feet
its ruby body stark against the rain-soaked patio
the graying wooden fence
the white saturated sky
is a greeting

crimson against the skin of my thighs
heavy droplets and watercolor stains
spreading on my underwear
was startling
but this was the red of dying
covering me in knowing
the growing thing was gone

it should scare me, this flash of red
but it doesn't
the cardinal picking seeds
from the ground after a hard rain
on a cold white morning
its beak is alive
its feet are alive
its wings take it to the top of the tree
where its mate is waiting

the living cannot scare me

I hope to see its bright
crimson body against the gray of the ash tree
that shivers in the late winter wind
like letting out a long-contained sigh

Excavations

After Ada Limón

In The Descent they took the way untraveled
                          deep into the lonely dark
look how that turned out for them...

          Being unmapped means—
doctors can only breach the interior by specialized vessels equipped
for
      tunnels of molten explosion,

uncontrolled bleeding,

they must intubate the hollow throat, excavating
the debris, separating magma from rock face

Never forget, I want to yell,
this is all born from the same violence!

How many others have been
                       explored

        against their will

all in the name of discovery

the wet cave

      of my body is more

beautiful in

solid

mystery

must you

crack it open

cave water

spilling out onto your hands

being unmapped means—

there is infinite space

to fill

room to grow secret

musty, quiet things

to be submerged

in the songs of all those lost

to the deep

timestream

whose current flows

backwards

      can't you hear them

singing

in   the   dark?

like letting out a long-contained sigh

My heart is

the long black hair
of a horse's tail
flowing out the back of a padlocked trailer
flirting with the wind on the highway
beckoning anyone to see it waving

Locket for the Dead

Victorian families wore lockets
with a coil of their love's hair
to keep them close
to their hearts

Now the mementos of the dead are digital
recordings of their dying breath
      ventilator bedside goodbyes
      bloodied Palestinian children pulled from
          collapsed homes
      people with their faces pressed to the pavement,
          cop knees on their neck
      flooded homes sweeping people away
          and all the dead we do not see

We should be made to wear a locket
heavy with the hair of the dead
boring us into the ground, so heavy we can't
meet each other's eyes
make us stumble and reach for one another

They would rather us remove our tear ducts
carve out the will to care

      memory resets at the speed of the next scroll

There are no monuments vast enough
to cover the bloodstains of this nation
gripping us tight in the imperial death machine
      except the moments
      those taken insisted on their own survival

      A child in Egypt presses her lips
      to a bottle filled with life-giving lentils

She whispers a prayer at the mouth
of this bottle
tossing it into the sea with hope
the waves will carry it to a family
in Gaza

If she remains relentlessly
committed to protecting the living
even when the crushing dark
could send her bottle floating
on forever

    what do we owe the living,
    every day they resist
    being made to watch over
    their own graves

Comorbidly Yours

You don't ask, "have you tried...?"
      We know better

Instead, dump your bag out on the table
      out spills
  hand sanitizer
      face masks/ in a rainbow array
a HEPA filter, a beacon of purple UV light
     hand warmers for this chilly day
nasal sprays ("take one, I have extra")
    oils for calming
oils for dry skin
    oils for the joints
a magical exchange of remedies/ from
the whisper network in the land of the ill

Medical blue gloved hands come disembodied
from a room that won't meet your eyes
but wants you to slip that mask down
just to see your grimace

Care comes from the hands of beloved
coconspirators bringing tea
to the table
Being outside with you, sweating or chilled
     is a miracle
you always send me on my way
with gifts
stickers you made yourself
    a handful of figs from your yard
bluebonnets to plant early and wait
    We won't see them grow for another year
or two

but everything planted takes root
breathing hard under hot packed earth

life happens here
        the whispers that grow louder
        each time we press our smiles
        against each other's heart windows
they're reserved, conserved, for those who can
feel them even behind the mask

«Work to help you reconnect to your body»

The following works were instrumental in helping me to heal, to work towards forgiveness and radical acceptance of my body, and to begin to write my stories and share them with others. I hope that they can be helpful for you too, and I share them in gratitude to these writers and creators who helped me on my journey of reconnecting with myself.

1. Your wound / my garden by Alok Vaid Menon
2. Always a Relic, Never a Reliquary by Kim Sousa
3. Wound from the Mouth of a Wound by Torrin A. Greathouse
4. The Most Spectacular Mistake by Anatalia Vallez
5. The Carrying by Ada Limón
6. Your Body is Not an Apology by Sonya Renee Taylor
7. I Had a Miscarriage: A Memoir, A Movement by Jessica Zucker
8. Body Work: The Radical Power of Personal Narrative by Melissa Febos
9. The Invisible Kingdom: Reimagining Chronic Illness by Megan O'Rourke
10. Lord of the Butterflies by Andrea Gibson
11. Pain Woman Takes Your Keys, and Other Essays from a Nervous System by Sonya Huber
12. Sick, a Memoir by Porochista Khakpour
13. Care Work: Dreaming Disability Justice by Leah Lakshmi Piepzna-Samarasinha
14. Disfigured: On Fairy Tales, Disability, and Making Space by Amanda Leduc
15. Love Is an Ex-Country by Randa Jarrar

Writing activities for reconnecting with your body»

Conversations with the body:

Write a persona poem or prose piece in the voice of your body, or an aspect of your physical self that you have hated, or not appreciated.

Honoring our origin stories:

What is the origin story of your body? Where do you begin? Where are you now? Write this origin in the style of a folktale, a fairy tale, a myth.

«Acknowledgements»

Thank you to Yael Valencia Aldana and the Purple Ink Press team for taking a chance on this tender little book.

Thank you to the following publications where these poems first appeared:

To the Chicon Street Poets Anthology for publishing "How Best May I Honor You."

To the NILVX Anthology for publishing "Altar."

To Public Poetry's Enough Anthology for publishing "The Graveyard of Good Health and for publishing 'Comorbidly Yours' in the Unbroken Anthology."

To PANK Latinx Archive for publishing "My Heart Is."

To West Trestle Review and Rio Grande Review for publishing "A Year of Offerings to the Body."

To the Infrarealista Review and Plancha Press for publishing my poem, "Beating Heart," in the Escritorio Purgatorio zine.

Thank you all of the wonderful writers who have participated in my Reconnecting to the Body writing workshop and inspired my work.

Much gratitude to the wonderful poets and friends who gave me feedback and helped me shape my work, including ire'ene lara silva, jo reyes-boitel, Cloud Delfina, Kim Sousa, Liz Clausen, Lindsey Carmichael Blackwell and many others.

All thanks to my chronically ill and disabled loves who always hold space for naps, hugs, being late, canceling plans and allowing me to be my most expansive, messy self.

To all of the women in my family who encouraged my words and my connection with my body, especially my grandmothers Paula and Ines, my cousins Beth and Trisha, my aunt Sherri and my mother Christi.

To Ramiro, my love and partner through all the joys, the heart-aches, the surgeries, the tears and laughter. You've been there for it all and I love you for walking this path with me.

ACKNOWLEDGEMENTS